Can You See
the Wind?

By Allan Fowler

Consultants

Linda Cornwell, Learning Resource Consultant,
Indiana Department of Education

Sharyn Fenwick, Elementary Science/Math Specialist,
Gustavus Adolphus College, St. Peter, Minnesota

Peter Goodwin, Science Teacher,
Kent School, Kent, Connecticut

⟨P⟩ Children's Press®
A Division of Grolier Publishing
New York   London   Hong Kong   Sydney
Danbury, Connecticut

Visit Children's Press® on the Internet at:
http://publishing.grolier.com

Designer: Herman Adler Design Group

Library of Congress Cataloging-in-Publication Data

Fowler, Allan.
    Can you see the wind? / by Allan Fowler.
      p. cm. – (Rookie read-about science)
    Includes index.
    Summary: A simple discussion of the wind, the causes of air movements,
and the uses of wind power.
    ISBN 0-516-20814-4 (lib. bdg.)   0-516-26479-6 (pbk.)
    1. Winds—Juvenile literature. [1. Winds.] I. Title. II. Series.
QC931.4.F68   1999   97-31277
551.51'8—dc21   CIP
                                       AC

Someone once said that
wind was air in a hurry.

On a very cold day, you
might think it's in too
much of a hurry.

Icy wind can seem to blow
right through you and
make you feel even colder.

Other winds are more
welcome. You need
wind to fly a kite or fill
the sails of a boat to
push it along the water.

Doesn't a cool breeze feel good on a hot summer day?

Sometimes people even make their own wind by waving a paper fan or turning on an electric fan.

How are nature's winds turned on? Why does air move from one place to another?

If every place on Earth were the same temperature at the same time, there would be no winds. But some places are warm while others are cold.

How Wind Is Made

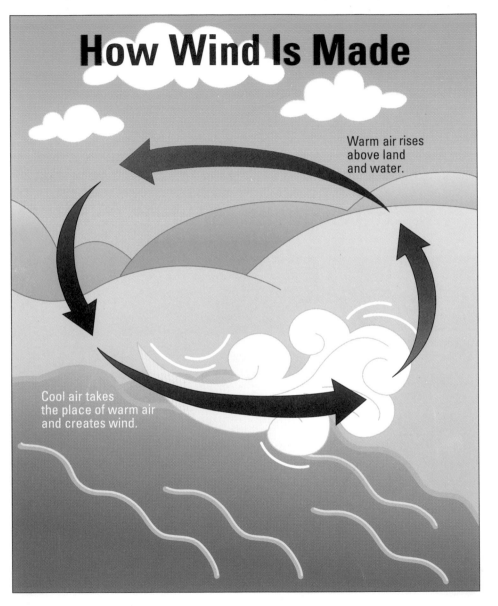

Warm air rises above land and water.

Cool air takes the place of warm air and creates wind.

When air is warm, it rises.
As it rises above land or
water, cooler air rushes
in to take its place.

That rush of air is wind.

Light winds are called
breezes. Strong winds
are called gales.

Tornadoes have the
strongest winds and
do great damage.

Tornadoes are also known
as twisters, because they
blow in a circle.

Hurricanes also produce strong winds.

A hurricane is a tropical storm that forms over a warm ocean.

Can you see the wind?
You can certainly see
some of the things it does.

Pollen is a powder that
must be carried from one
plant to another to help
new plants grow.

Wind carries the pollen
of grasses and most trees.

Wind blows desert sand
into hills called dunes.

Over a very long time, wind can even change the shape of rocks. Bit by tiny bit, it wears the rocks away.

Before people knew
how to use steam, gas,
or electricity for power,
they used the wind.

They crossed oceans in
great ships driven by wind.

21

People built windmills with big sails that turned in the wind. The windmills ground corn for bread or pumped water off flooded lands.

Many farms still use
windmills today.

Winds high in the sky
often blow much harder
than those at ground level.

A jet plane goes slower
if it has to fly against
the wind.

With the wind pushing
it from behind, however,
a plane might reach the
airport ahead of time.

Scientists send up weather balloons to learn how the wind is blowing.

Can you see the wind? Just
look up at the clouds. How
fast is the wind moving
them along? Where is the
wind coming from—north,
south, east, or west?

Closer to the ground, look
for a flag flapping or a
tree swaying in the breeze.

Yes, in a way, you can see the wind!

Words You Know

dunes

pollen

hurricane

tornado

weather balloon

windmills

31

Index

About the Author

Allan Fowler is a freelance writer with a background in advertising. Born in New York, he now lives in Chicago and enjoys traveling.

Photo Credits

©: Photo Researchers: cover (David Frazier), 4 (B & C Alexander), 3 (Frederick Ayer), 17 (Biophoto Associates), 13, 31 top left (Howard Bluestein), 26, 31 top right (Mark C. Burnett), 27 (Jim Corwin), 21 (Richard Divald), 23, 31 bottom (Lowell Georgia), 6 (Bruce Hayes), 7 (Deni & Will McIntyre), 29 (Earl Roberge), 8 (F. Stuart Westmorland), 17 inset, 30 top right (Jerome Wexler); Viesti Collection, Inc.: 18, 30 top left (IBL), 22, 28 (Bavaria), 19 (Alan Kearney), 24 (Valder/Tormey), 14, 30 bottom (Kevin Vandivier), 9 (Robert Winslow).

Diagram on page 10: Lee Glynn